Yes, Sister!

No, Sister!

cartoons by
Joe Lane

published by About Comics, Camarillo, California

Yes, Sister! No, Sister!
Originally published by Michael Book Co., 1956
About Comics edition published April, 2018

Customized editions available

Send all queries to *questions@aboutcomics.com*

"Jam session, anyone?"

"Oh, we never have school on St. Patrick's day!"

"One thing you'll find out—they're all born with concupiscence."

"I hear her folks are well off . . ."

"We'll start off with a cocktail . . .

. . . Shrimp, that is!"

"This looks like my room after one of our kindergarten parties!"

"Look, Sister . . . Captain Hook!"

"I'll be glad to help you with your problem . . ."

NOVICE
INVESTURE
CEREMONY

"I don't care what he says about the low pressure area and the high pressure area, my corns forecast rain!"

"Ludmilla, here in the Novitiate we strive to treat our postulants with deference, tenderness and understanding . . . and, if an occasion warrants . . . to mete out justice with kindness and clarity . . .

. . . So . . . what's the beef?"

"Sister will see you, Father, as soon as she's finished with Bishop Sheen."

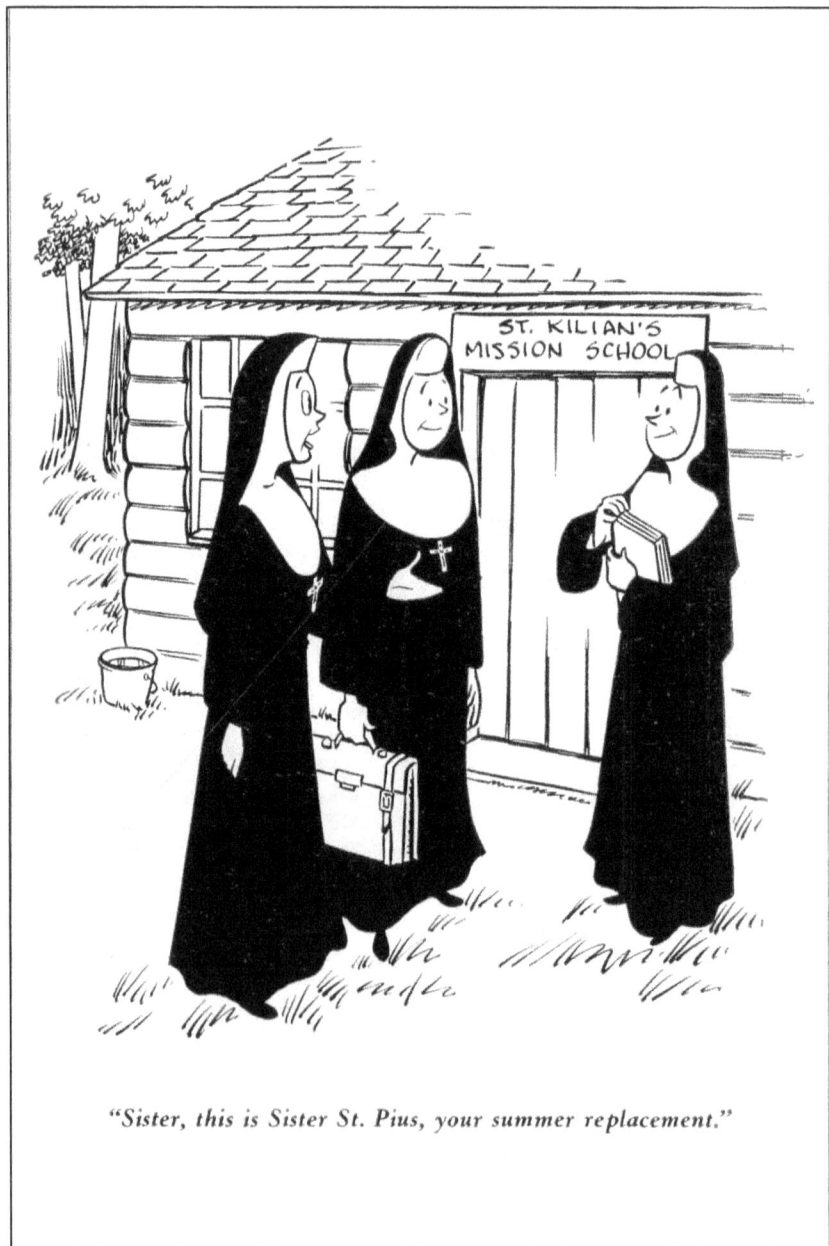

"Sister, this is Sister St. Pius, your summer replacement."

"I'm spending my vacation down in the South American missions. How's about you?"

"Sister's real proud of me, Mom. She says I'm quite an ordeal!"

"They're twenty-five cents a chance . . . five for a dollar!"

"The latest poll shows 5 for Marian blue, 4 want angel white, 6 for papal yellow, 3 for cherub pink . . ."

"*Quite a relief from those crowded classrooms in the States!*"

". . . 'Take it easy, avoid excitement,' " he says. "I'd like to see him *with a room full of sixth graders!*"

"So long, neighbors!"

"Look, Mom and Dad, my winter, spring, summer and fall outfit!"

"We've come to render to Caesar!"

"Sister knows so much about Lincoln, he must have been in her class!"

"Meet your darling exemption!"

"Uh 1, uh 2, uh 3 . . ."

"Thank you, Sister. Now is there anyone else there with you?"

"I won't be out today, guys . . ."

"I have a previous commitment."

"If you guys ever need a lie detector . . ."

"Well, Adams, so far so good."

"I believe we may safely assume, Doctor, that Mickey has recovered the will to live."

"Since we got our TV set, we rarely use our record player."

"Young man, are you in the state of grace?"

"Thank Heaven! Home at last!!"

". . . Er, is the lady of the house in?"

"Cease and desist with the jazz Music for Tonight, and get going on the classical practicing for today!"

"And may we assume that radio, heater, seat covers, power steering, power brakes and their ilk are included in your fabulous full price of $50?"

"To whom do we pray to get a refrigerator like that?"

"Sisters, the latest book on metaphysics is being reviewed at this time on the educational channel!"

"Oh, oh! Muzynski's gone back to watching the late, late, late show!"

"Get thee behind me!"

"All I asked was—'Sister, will you bait the hook?'"

"Do you have a steady job, Sister?"

"My word! She's quite a flapper!"

"You have eight wrong, Thaddeus. Would you care to try for sixteen?"

"I wouldn't be too concerned, Mr. Strebler. About this time next week, come three a.m., and you'll be sure his lungs are perfect."

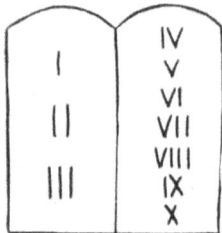

"Gee whiz, Sister! After we learn these, life ain't gonna be the same!"

"I just can't seem to get his confidence!"

"*Good news, Mr. Daray. The doctor says you can go home tomorrow to your wife and the ten little Darays!*"

"*Well, fiddle dee dee!*"

"Could you suggest something for a Mother General?"

"Is Itty Bitty Buddy Boy striving for a zero?"

"I don't want to be a brilliant woman, Sister. I want to be a nun, like you!"

"The poor marks, Antonson. Pourquois?"

"For me, *this* is *a light collation!*"

"According to this, I didn't even reach the first plateau!"

"Mrs. Kerr, why aren't you a nun?"

"You're doin' a bang-up job wit' Lawrence, Sister Mary.
Ev'ry night he reads me the funnies!"

"From our Do-It-Yourself Club, Sister Allen. A token of our esteem!"

"How do you do, Sister? You doubtlessly have been spending a great deal of time wondering about the qualifications of our party candidates . . ."

"Come in, Reverend Mother. We're having a bull session!"

Get all our little books of Joe Lane's little nuns

Our Little Nuns
More Little Nuns
Nuns So Lovable
Vale of Dears
Yes, Sister! No, Sister!

or get

The Big Book of Nun Cartoons
a lifetime supply all in one volume!

Look for them where you got this book,
or visit www.AboutComics.com

Classic Cartoon Collections!

Sam Brier's 1950s quirky comic strip is about kids playing as adults... or adults drawn as kids.

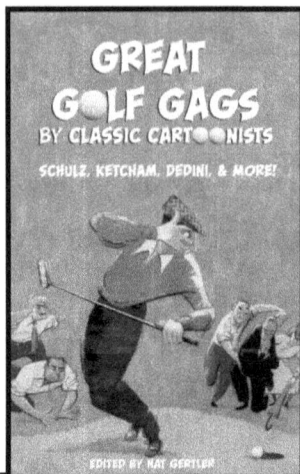

Golf cartoons by Hank Ketcham, Eldon Dedini, Virgil Partch, Bill O'Malley, & more

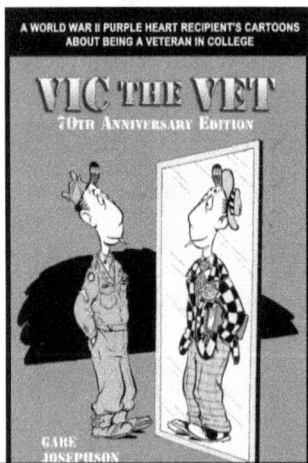

Cartoons about being a World War II vet at college on the GI Bill... by a World War II vet while at college.

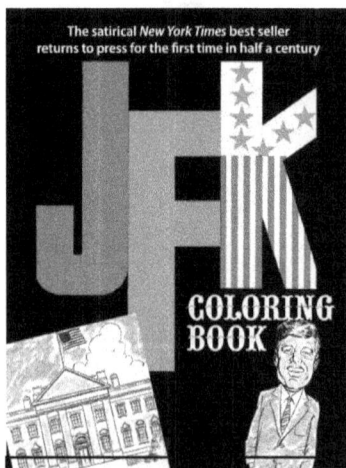

Mort Drucker illustrates this New York Times best-seller